BABY SHOWER FOR:

_____

_____

Stick your favorite
picture here

Guests

Name:_____

Parenting Advice

_____
_____
_____
_____
_____
_____

Wishes for Baby

_____
_____
_____
_____
_____

Resemblance

☐ Mostly Mom   ☐ Definitely Dad

I hope the baby gets Moms:_____

I hope the baby gets Dads:_____

Predictions

Eye Color: _____   Hair Color:_____

Length:_____   Weight:_____

D.O.B:_____   Time:_____

Labor will last: ___Days ___Hours ___Mins

Guests

Name:_____

Parenting Advice

_____
_____
_____
_____
_____
_____

Wishes for Baby

_____
_____
_____
_____
_____

Resemblance

☐ Mostly Mom   ☐ Definitely Dad

I hope the baby gets Moms:_____

I hope the baby gets Dads:_____

Predictions

Eye Color: _____   Hair Color:_____

Length:_____   Weight:_____

D.O.B:_____   Time:_____

Labor will last: ___Days ___Hours ___Mins

Guests

Name:_____

Parenting Advice

_____
_____
_____
_____
_____
_____

Wishes for Baby

_____
_____
_____
_____
_____
_____

Resemblance

☐ Mostly Mom   ☐ Definitely Dad

I hope the baby gets Moms:_____

I hope the baby gets Dads:_____

Predictions

Eye Color: _____   Hair Color:_____

Length:_____   Weight:_____

D.O.B:_____   Time:_____

Labor will last: ___Days ___Hours ___Mins

Guests

Name:_____

Parenting Advice

_____
_____
_____
_____
_____

Wishes for Baby

_____
_____
_____
_____
_____

Resemblance

☐ Mostly Mom   ☐ Definitely Dad

I hope the baby gets Moms:_____

I hope the baby gets Dads:_____

Predictions

Eye Color: _____   Hair Color:_____

Length:_____   Weight:_____

D.O.B:_____   Time:_____

Labor will last: ___Days ___Hours ___Mins

Guests

Name:_____

Parenting Advice

_____
_____
_____
_____
_____
_____

Wishes for Baby

_____
_____
_____
_____
_____

Resemblance

☐ Mostly Mom   ☐ Definitely Dad

I hope the baby gets Moms:_____

I hope the baby gets Dads:_____

Predictions

Eye Color: _____   Hair Color:_____

Length:_____   Weight:_____

D.O.B:_____   Time:_____

Labor will last: ___Days ___Hours ___Mins

Guests

Name:_____

Parenting Advice

_____
_____
_____
_____
_____
_____

Wishes for Baby

_____
_____
_____
_____
_____
_____

Resemblance

☐ Mostly Mom   ☐ Definitely Dad

I hope the baby gets Moms:_____

I hope the baby gets Dads:_____

Predictions

Eye Color: _____   Hair Color:_____

Length:_____   Weight:_____

D.O.B:_____   Time:_____

Labor will last: ___Days ___Hours ___Mins

Guests

Name:_____

Parenting Advice

_____
_____
_____
_____
_____
_____

Wishes for Baby

_____
_____
_____
_____
_____

Resemblance

☐ Mostly Mom   ☐ Definitely Dad

I hope the baby gets Moms:_____

I hope the baby gets Dads:_____

Predictions

Eye Color: _____   Hair Color:_____

Length:_____   Weight:_____

D.O.B:_____   Time:_____

Labor will last: ___Days ___Hours ___Mins

Guests

Name:_____

Parenting Advice

_____
_____
_____
_____

Wishes for Baby

_____
_____
_____
_____
_____

Resemblance

☐ Mostly Mom   ☐ Definitely Dad

I hope the baby gets Moms:_____

I hope the baby gets Dads:_____

Predictions

Eye Color: _____   Hair Color:_____

Length:_____   Weight:_____

D.O.B:_____   Time:_____

Labor will last: ___Days ___Hours ___Mins

Guests

Name:_____

Parenting Advice

_____
_____
_____
_____
_____
_____

Wishes for Baby

_____
_____
_____
_____
_____
_____

Resemblance

☐ Mostly Mom   ☐ Definitely Dad

I hope the baby gets Moms:_____

I hope the baby gets Dads:_____

Predictions

Eye Color: _____   Hair Color:_____

Length:_____   Weight:_____

D.O.B:_____   Time:_____

Labor will last: ___Days ___Hours ___Mins

Guests

Name:_____

Parenting Advice

_____
_____
_____
_____
_____
_____

Wishes for Baby

_____
_____
_____
_____
_____
_____

Resemblance

☐ Mostly Mom   ☐ Definitely Dad

I hope the baby gets Moms:_____

I hope the baby gets Dads:_____

Predictions

Eye Color: _____   Hair Color:_____

Length:_____   Weight:_____

D.O.B:_____   Time:_____

Labor will last: ___Days ___Hours ___Mins

Guests

Name:_____

Parenting Advice

_____
_____
_____
_____
_____
_____

Wishes for Baby

_____
_____
_____
_____
_____
_____

Resemblance

☐ Mostly Mom   ☐ Definitely Dad

I hope the baby gets Moms:_____

I hope the baby gets Dads:_____

Predictions

Eye Color: _____   Hair Color:_____

Length:_____   Weight:_____

D.O.B:_____   Time:_____

Labor will last: ___Days ___Hours ___Mins

Guests

Name:_____

Parenting Advice

_____
_____
_____
_____
_____

Wishes for Baby

_____
_____
_____
_____
_____

Resemblance

☐ Mostly Mom   ☐ Definitely Dad

I hope the baby gets Moms:_____

I hope the baby gets Dads:_____

Predictions

Eye Color: _____   Hair Color:_____

Length:_____   Weight:_____

D.O.B:_____   Time:_____

Labor will last: ___Days ___Hours ___Mins

Guests

Name:_____

Parenting Advice

Wishes for Baby

Resemblance

☐ Mostly Mom   ☐ Definitely Dad

I hope the baby gets Moms:_____

I hope the baby gets Dads:_____

Predictions

Eye Color: _____   Hair Color:_____

Length:_____   Weight:_____

D.O.B:_____   Time:_____

Labor will last: ___Days ___Hours ___Mins

Guests

Name:_____

Parenting Advice

_____
_____
_____
_____
_____
_____

Wishes for Baby

_____
_____
_____
_____
_____

Resemblance

☐ Mostly Mom   ☐ Definitely Dad

I hope the baby gets Moms:_____

I hope the baby gets Dads:_____

Predictions

Eye Color: _____   Hair Color:_____

Length:_____   Weight:_____

D.O.B:_____   Time:_____

Labor will last: ___Days ___Hours ___Mins

Guests

Name:_____

Parenting Advice

_____
_____
_____
_____
_____
_____

Wishes for Baby

_____
_____
_____
_____
_____

Resemblance

☐ Mostly Mom   ☐ Definitely Dad

I hope the baby gets Moms:_____

I hope the baby gets Dads:_____

Predictions

Eye Color: _____   Hair Color:_____

Length:_____   Weight:_____

D.O.B:_____   Time:_____

Labor will last: ___Days ___Hours ___Mins

Guests

Name:_____

Parenting Advice

Wishes for Baby

Resemblance

☐ Mostly Mom   ☐ Definitely Dad

I hope the baby gets Moms:_____

I hope the baby gets Dads:_____

Predictions

Eye Color: _____   Hair Color:_____

Length:_____   Weight:_____

D.O.B:_____   Time:_____

Labor will last: ___Days ___Hours ___Mins

Guests

Name:_____

Parenting Advice

_____
_____
_____
_____
_____
_____

Wishes for Baby

_____
_____
_____
_____
_____

Resemblance

☐ Mostly Mom   ☐ Definitely Dad

I hope the baby gets Moms:_____

I hope the baby gets Dads:_____

Predictions

Eye Color: _____   Hair Color:_____

Length:_____   Weight:_____

D.O.B:_____   Time:_____

Labor will last: ___Days ___Hours ___Mins

Guests

Name:_____

Parenting Advice

_____
_____
_____
_____
_____
_____

Wishes for Baby

_____
_____
_____
_____
_____
_____

Resemblance

☐ Mostly Mom   ☐ Definitely Dad

I hope the baby gets Moms:_____

I hope the baby gets Dads:_____

Predictions

Eye Color: _____   Hair Color:_____

Length:_____   Weight:_____

D.O.B:_____   Time:_____

Labor will last: ___Days ___Hours ___Mins

Guests

Name:_____

Parenting Advice

_____
_____
_____
_____
_____

Wishes for Baby

_____
_____
_____
_____
_____

Resemblance

☐ Mostly Mom   ☐ Definitely Dad

I hope the baby gets Moms:_____

I hope the baby gets Dads:_____

Predictions

Eye Color: _____   Hair Color:_____

Length:_____   Weight:_____

D.O.B:_____   Time:_____

Labor will last: ___Days ___Hours ___Mins

Guests

Name:_____

Parenting Advice

_____
_____
_____
_____
_____

Wishes for Baby

_____
_____
_____
_____
_____

Resemblance

☐ Mostly Mom   ☐ Definitely Dad

I hope the baby gets Moms:_____

I hope the baby gets Dads:_____

Predictions

Eye Color: _____   Hair Color:_____

Length:_____   Weight:_____

D.O.B:_____   Time:_____

Labor will last: ___Days ___Hours ___Mins

Guests

Name:_____

Parenting Advice

_____
_____
_____
_____
_____
_____

Wishes for Baby

_____
_____
_____
_____
_____
_____

Resemblance

☐ Mostly Mom   ☐ Definitely Dad

I hope the baby gets Moms:_____

I hope the baby gets Dads:_____

Predictions

Eye Color: _____   Hair Color:_____

Length:_____   Weight:_____

D.O.B:_____   Time:_____

Labor will last: ___Days ___Hours ___Mins

Guests

Name:_____

Parenting Advice

_____
_____
_____
_____
_____
_____

Wishes for Baby

_____
_____

_____
_____
_____

Resemblance

☐ Mostly Mom   ☐ Definitely Dad

I hope the baby gets Moms:_____

I hope the baby gets Dads:_____

Predictions

Eye Color: _____   Hair Color:_____

Length:_____   Weight:_____

D.O.B:_____   Time:_____

Labor will last: ___Days ___Hours ___Mins

Guests

Name:_____

Parenting Advice

_____
_____
_____
_____
_____
_____

Wishes for Baby

_____
_____
_____
_____
_____
_____

Resemblance

☐ Mostly Mom   ☐ Definitely Dad

I hope the baby gets Moms:_____

I hope the baby gets Dads:_____

Predictions

Eye Color: _____   Hair Color:_____

Length:_____   Weight:_____

D.O.B:_____   Time:_____

Labor will last: ___Days ___Hours ___Mins

Guests

Name:_____

Parenting Advice

Wishes for Baby

Resemblance

☐ Mostly Mom   ☐ Definitely Dad

I hope the baby gets Moms:_____

I hope the baby gets Dads:_____

Predictions

Eye Color: _____   Hair Color:_____

Length:_____   Weight:_____

D.O.B:_____   Time:_____

Labor will last: ___Days ___Hours ___Mins

Guests

Name:_____

Parenting Advice

_____
_____
_____
_____
_____
_____

Wishes for Baby

_____
_____
_____
_____
_____

Resemblance

☐ Mostly Mom   ☐ Definitely Dad

I hope the baby gets Moms:_____

I hope the baby gets Dads:_____

Predictions

Eye Color: _____   Hair Color:_____

Length:_____   Weight:_____

D.O.B:_____   Time:_____

Labor will last: ___Days ___Hours ___Mins

Guests

Name:_____

Parenting Advice

_____
_____
_____
_____
_____
_____

Wishes for Baby

_____
_____
_____
_____
_____
_____

Resemblance

☐ Mostly Mom   ☐ Definitely Dad

I hope the baby gets Moms:_____

I hope the baby gets Dads:_____

Predictions

Eye Color: _____   Hair Color:_____

Length:_____   Weight:_____

D.O.B:_____   Time:_____

Labor will last: ___Days ___Hours ___Mins

Guests

Name:_____

Parenting Advice

_____
_____
_____
_____
_____
_____

Wishes for Baby

_____
_____
_____
_____
_____
_____

Resemblance

☐ Mostly Mom   ☐ Definitely Dad

I hope the baby gets Moms:_____

I hope the baby gets Dads:_____

Predictions

Eye Color: _____   Hair Color:_____

Length:_____   Weight:_____

D.O.B:_____   Time:_____

Labor will last: ___Days ___Hours ___Mins

Guests

Name:_____

Parenting Advice

_____
_____
_____
_____
_____
_____

Wishes for Baby

_____
_____
_____
_____
_____
_____

Resemblance

☐ Mostly Mom   ☐ Definitely Dad

I hope the baby gets Moms:_____

I hope the baby gets Dads:_____

Predictions

Eye Color: _____   Hair Color:_____

Length:_____   Weight:_____

D.O.B:_____   Time:_____

Labor will last: ___Days ___Hours ___Mins

Guests

Name:_____

Parenting Advice

_____
_____
_____
_____
_____
_____

Wishes for Baby

_____
_____
_____
_____
_____

Resemblance

☐ Mostly Mom   ☐ Definitely Dad

I hope the baby gets Moms:_____

I hope the baby gets Dads:_____

Predictions

Eye Color: _____   Hair Color:_____

Length:_____   Weight:_____

D.O.B:_____   Time:_____

Labor will last: ___Days ___Hours ___Mins

Guests

Name:_____

Parenting Advice

_____
_____
_____
_____
_____
_____

Wishes for Baby

_____
_____
_____
_____
_____
_____

Resemblance

☐ Mostly Mom   ☐ Definitely Dad

I hope the baby gets Moms:_____

I hope the baby gets Dads:_____

Predictions

Eye Color: _____   Hair Color:_____

Length:_____   Weight:_____

D.O.B:_____   Time:_____

Labor will last: ___Days ___Hours ___Mins

Guests

Name:_____

Parenting Advice

_____
_____
_____
_____
_____
_____

Wishes for Baby

_____
_____
_____
_____
_____

Resemblance

☐ Mostly Mom   ☐ Definitely Dad

I hope the baby gets Moms:_____

I hope the baby gets Dads:_____

Predictions

Eye Color: _____   Hair Color:_____

Length:_____   Weight:_____

D.O.B:_____   Time:_____

Labor will last: ___Days ___Hours ___Mins

Guests

Name:_____

Parenting Advice

Wishes for Baby

Resemblance

☐ Mostly Mom   ☐ Definitely Dad

I hope the baby gets Moms:_____

I hope the baby gets Dads:_____

Predictions

Eye Color: _____   Hair Color:_____

Length:_____   Weight:_____

D.O.B:_____   Time:_____

Labor will last: ___Days ___Hours ___Mins

Guests

Name:_____

Parenting Advice

_____
_____
_____
_____
_____
_____

Wishes for Baby

_____
_____
_____
_____
_____
_____

Resemblance

☐ Mostly Mom   ☐ Definitely Dad

I hope the baby gets Moms:_____

I hope the baby gets Dads:_____

Predictions

Eye Color: _____   Hair Color:_____

Length:_____   Weight:_____

D.O.B:_____   Time:_____

Labor will last: ___Days ___Hours ___Mins

Guests

Name:_____

Parenting Advice

_____
_____
_____
_____
_____
_____

Wishes for Baby

_____
_____
_____
_____
_____

Resemblance

☐ Mostly Mom   ☐ Definitely Dad

I hope the baby gets Moms:_____

I hope the baby gets Dads:_____

Predictions

Eye Color: _____   Hair Color:_____

Length:_____   Weight:_____

D.O.B:_____   Time:_____

Labor will last: ___Days ___Hours ___Mins

Guests

Name:_____

Parenting Advice

_____
_____
_____
_____
_____
_____

Wishes for Baby

_____
_____
_____
_____
_____

Resemblance

☐ Mostly Mom   ☐ Definitely Dad

I hope the baby gets Moms:_____

I hope the baby gets Dads:_____

Predictions

Eye Color: _____   Hair Color:_____

Length:_____   Weight:_____

D.O.B:_____   Time:_____

Labor will last: ___Days ___Hours ___Mins

Guests

Name:_____

Parenting Advice

_____
_____
_____
_____
_____
_____

Wishes for Baby

_____
_____
_____
_____
_____

Resemblance

☐ Mostly Mom   ☐ Definitely Dad

I hope the baby gets Moms:_____

I hope the baby gets Dads:_____

Predictions

Eye Color: _____   Hair Color:_____

Length:_____   Weight:_____

D.O.B:_____   Time:_____

Labor will last: ___Days ___Hours ___Mins

Guests

Name:_____

Parenting Advice

_____
_____
_____
_____
_____
_____

Wishes for Baby

_____
_____
_____
_____
_____

Resemblance

☐ Mostly Mom   ☐ Definitely Dad

I hope the baby gets Moms:_____

I hope the baby gets Dads:_____

Predictions

Eye Color: _____   Hair Color:_____

Length:_____   Weight:_____

D.O.B:_____   Time:_____

Labor will last: ___Days ___Hours ___Mins

Guests

Name:_____

Parenting Advice

_____
_____
_____
_____
_____
_____

Wishes for Baby

_____
_____
_____
_____
_____

Resemblance

☐ Mostly Mom   ☐ Definitely Dad

I hope the baby gets Moms:_____

I hope the baby gets Dads:_____

Predictions

Eye Color: _____   Hair Color:_____

Length:_____   Weight:_____

D.O.B:_____   Time:_____

Labor will last: ___Days ___Hours ___Mins

Guests

Name:_____

Parenting Advice

_____
_____
_____
_____
_____
_____

Wishes for Baby

_____
_____
_____
_____
_____
_____

Resemblance

☐ Mostly Mom   ☐ Definitely Dad

I hope the baby gets Moms:_____

I hope the baby gets Dads:_____

Predictions

Eye Color: _____   Hair Color:_____

Length:_____   Weight:_____

D.O.B:_____   Time:_____

Labor will last: ___Days ___Hours ___Mins

Guests

Name:_____

Parenting Advice

_____
_____
_____
_____
_____
_____

Wishes for Baby

_____
_____
_____
_____
_____

Resemblance

☐ Mostly Mom   ☐ Definitely Dad

I hope the baby gets Moms:_____

I hope the baby gets Dads:_____

Predictions

Eye Color: _____   Hair Color:_____

Length:_____   Weight:_____

D.O.B:_____   Time:_____

Labor will last: ___Days ___Hours ___Mins

Guests

Name:_____

Parenting Advice

_____
_____
_____
_____
_____
_____

Wishes for Baby

_____
_____
_____
_____
_____

Resemblance

☐ Mostly Mom   ☐ Definitely Dad

I hope the baby gets Moms:_____

I hope the baby gets Dads:_____

Predictions

Eye Color: _____   Hair Color:_____

Length:_____   Weight:_____

D.O.B:_____   Time:_____

Labor will last: ___Days ___Hours ___Mins

Guests

Name:_____

Parenting Advice

_____
_____
_____
_____
_____
_____

Wishes for Baby

_____
_____
_____
_____
_____

Resemblance

☐ Mostly Mom   ☐ Definitely Dad

I hope the baby gets Moms:_____

I hope the baby gets Dads:_____

Predictions

Eye Color: _____   Hair Color:_____

Length:_____   Weight:_____

D.O.B:_____   Time:_____

Labor will last: ___Days ___Hours ___Mins

Guests

Name:_____

Parenting Advice

_____
_____
_____
_____
_____

Wishes for Baby

_____
_____
_____
_____
_____

Resemblance

☐ Mostly Mom   ☐ Definitely Dad

I hope the baby gets Moms:_____

I hope the baby gets Dads:_____

Predictions

Eye Color: _____   Hair Color:_____

Length:_____   Weight:_____

D.O.B:_____   Time:_____

Labor will last: ___Days ___Hours ___Mins

Guests

Name:_____

Parenting Advice

_____
_____
_____
_____
_____
_____

Wishes for Baby

_____
_____
_____
_____
_____
_____

Resemblance

☐ Mostly Mom   ☐ Definitely Dad

I hope the baby gets Moms:_____

I hope the baby gets Dads:_____

Predictions

Eye Color: _____   Hair Color:_____

Length:_____   Weight:_____

D.O.B:_____   Time:_____

Labor will last: ___Days ___Hours ___Mins

Guests

Name:_____

Parenting Advice

_____
_____
_____
_____
_____
_____

Wishes for Baby

_____
_____
_____
_____
_____
_____

Resemblance

☐ Mostly Mom   ☐ Definitely Dad

I hope the baby gets Moms:_____

I hope the baby gets Dads:_____

Predictions

Eye Color: _____   Hair Color:_____

Length:_____   Weight:_____

D.O.B:_____   Time:_____

Labor will last: ___Days ___Hours ___Mins

Guests

Name:_____

Parenting Advice

_____
_____
_____
_____
_____
_____

Wishes for Baby

_____
_____
_____
_____
_____

Resemblance

☐ Mostly Mom   ☐ Definitely Dad

I hope the baby gets Moms:_____

I hope the baby gets Dads:_____

Predictions

Eye Color: _____   Hair Color:_____

Length:_____   Weight:_____

D.O.B:_____   Time:_____

Labor will last: ___Days ___Hours ___Mins

Guests

Name:_____

Parenting Advice

_____
_____
_____
_____
_____
_____

Wishes for Baby

_____
_____
_____
_____
_____
_____

Resemblance

☐ Mostly Mom   ☐ Definitely Dad

I hope the baby gets Moms:_____

I hope the baby gets Dads:_____

Predictions

Eye Color: _____   Hair Color:_____

Length:_____   Weight:_____

D.O.B:_____   Time:_____

Labor will last: ___Days ___Hours ___Mins

Guests

Name:_____

Parenting Advice

Wishes for Baby

Resemblance

☐ Mostly Mom   ☐ Definitely Dad

I hope the baby gets Moms:_____

I hope the baby gets Dads:_____

Predictions

Eye Color: _____   Hair Color:_____

Length:_____   Weight:_____

D.O.B:_____   Time:_____

Labor will last: ___Days ___Hours ___Mins

Guests

Name:_____

Parenting Advice

_____
_____
_____
_____
_____
_____

Wishes for Baby

_____
_____
_____
_____
_____
_____

Resemblance

☐ Mostly Mom   ☐ Definitely Dad

I hope the baby gets Moms:_____

I hope the baby gets Dads:_____

Predictions

Eye Color: _____   Hair Color:_____

Length:_____   Weight:_____

D.O.B:_____   Time:_____

Labor will last: ___Days ___Hours ___Mins

Guests

Name:_____

Parenting Advice

_____
_____
_____
_____
_____
_____

Wishes for Baby

_____
_____
_____
_____
_____
_____

Resemblance

☐ Mostly Mom   ☐ Definitely Dad

I hope the baby gets Moms:_____

I hope the baby gets Dads:_____

Predictions

Eye Color: _____   Hair Color:_____

Length:_____   Weight:_____

D.O.B:_____   Time:_____

Labor will last: ___Days ___Hours ___Mins

Guests

Name:_____

Parenting Advice

_____
_____
_____
_____
_____
_____

Wishes for Baby

_____
_____
_____
_____
_____

Resemblance

☐ Mostly Mom   ☐ Definitely Dad

I hope the baby gets Moms:_____

I hope the baby gets Dads:_____

Predictions

Eye Color: _____   Hair Color:_____

Length:_____   Weight:_____

D.O.B:_____   Time:_____

Labor will last: ___Days ___Hours ___Mins

Guests

Name:_____

Parenting Advice

_____
_____
_____
_____

Wishes for Baby

_____
_____
_____
_____
_____

Resemblance

☐ Mostly Mom   ☐ Definitely Dad

I hope the baby gets Moms:_____

I hope the baby gets Dads:_____

Predictions

Eye Color: _____   Hair Color:_____

Length:_____   Weight:_____

D.O.B:_____   Time:_____

Labor will last: ___Days ___Hours ___Mins

Guests

Name:_____

Parenting Advice

_____
_____
_____
_____
_____
_____

Wishes for Baby

_____
_____
_____
_____
_____

Resemblance

☐ Mostly Mom   ☐ Definitely Dad

I hope the baby gets Moms:_____

I hope the baby gets Dads:_____

Predictions

Eye Color: _____   Hair Color:_____

Length:_____   Weight:_____

D.O.B:_____   Time:_____

Labor will last: ___Days ___Hours ___Mins

Guests

Name:_____

Parenting Advice

_____
_____
_____
_____
_____
_____

Wishes for Baby

_____
_____
_____
_____
_____

Resemblance

☐ Mostly Mom   ☐ Definitely Dad

I hope the baby gets Moms:_____

I hope the baby gets Dads:_____

Predictions

Eye Color: _____   Hair Color:_____

Length:_____   Weight:_____

D.O.B:_____   Time:_____

Labor will last: ___Days ___Hours ___Mins

Guests

Name:_____

Parenting Advice

_____
_____
_____
_____
_____
_____

Wishes for Baby

_____
_____
_____
_____
_____

Resemblance

☐ Mostly Mom   ☐ Definitely Dad

I hope the baby gets Moms:_____

I hope the baby gets Dads:_____

Predictions

Eye Color: _____   Hair Color:_____

Length:_____   Weight:_____

D.O.B:_____   Time:_____

Labor will last: ___Days ___Hours ___Mins

Guests

Name:_____

Parenting Advice

_____
_____
_____
_____
_____
_____

Wishes for Baby

_____
_____
_____
_____
_____
_____

Resemblance

☐ Mostly Mom   ☐ Definitely Dad

I hope the baby gets Moms:_____

I hope the baby gets Dads:_____

Predictions

Eye Color: _____   Hair Color:_____

Length:_____   Weight:_____

D.O.B:_____   Time:_____

Labor will last: ___Days ___Hours ___Mins

Guests

Name:_____

Parenting Advice

_____
_____
_____
_____
_____
_____

Wishes for Baby

_____
_____
_____
_____
_____

Resemblance

☐ Mostly Mom   ☐ Definitely Dad

I hope the baby gets Moms:_____

I hope the baby gets Dads:_____

Predictions

Eye Color: _____   Hair Color:_____

Length:_____   Weight:_____

D.O.B:_____   Time:_____

Labor will last: ___Days ___Hours ___Mins

Guests

Name:_____

Parenting Advice

_____
_____
_____
_____
_____
_____

Wishes for Baby

_____
_____
_____
_____
_____

Resemblance

☐ Mostly Mom   ☐ Definitely Dad

I hope the baby gets Moms:_____

I hope the baby gets Dads:_____

Predictions

Eye Color: _____   Hair Color:_____

Length:_____   Weight:_____

D.O.B:_____   Time:_____

Labor will last: ___Days ___Hours ___Mins

Guests

Name:_____

Parenting Advice

_____
_____
_____
_____
_____

Wishes for Baby

_____
_____
_____
_____
_____

Resemblance

☐ Mostly Mom   ☐ Definitely Dad

I hope the baby gets Moms:_____

I hope the baby gets Dads:_____

Predictions

Eye Color: _____   Hair Color:_____

Length:_____   Weight:_____

D.O.B:_____   Time:_____

Labor will last: ___Days ___Hours ___Mins

Guests

Name:_____

Parenting Advice

Wishes for Baby

Resemblance

☐ Mostly Mom   ☐ Definitely Dad

I hope the baby gets Moms:_____

I hope the baby gets Dads:_____

Predictions

Eye Color: _____   Hair Color:_____

Length:_____   Weight:_____

D.O.B:_____   Time:_____

Labor will last: ___Days ___Hours ___Mins

Guests

Name:_____

Parenting Advice

Wishes for Baby

Resemblance

☐ Mostly Mom   ☐ Definitely Dad

I hope the baby gets Moms:_____

I hope the baby gets Dads:_____

Predictions

Eye Color: _____   Hair Color:_____

Length:_____   Weight:_____

D.O.B:_____   Time:_____

Labor will last: ___Days ___Hours ___Mins

Guests

Name:_____

Parenting Advice

_____
_____
_____
_____
_____
_____

Wishes for Baby

_____
_____
_____
_____
_____
_____

Resemblance

☐ Mostly Mom   ☐ Definitely Dad

I hope the baby gets Moms:_____

I hope the baby gets Dads:_____

Predictions

Eye Color: _____   Hair Color:_____

Length:_____   Weight:_____

D.O.B:_____   Time:_____

Labor will last: ___Days ___Hours ___Mins

Guests

Name:_____

Parenting Advice

_____
_____
_____
_____
_____
_____

Wishes for Baby

_____
_____
_____
_____
_____
_____

Resemblance

☐ Mostly Mom   ☐ Definitely Dad

I hope the baby gets Moms:_____

I hope the baby gets Dads:_____

Predictions

Eye Color: _____   Hair Color:_____

Length:_____   Weight:_____

D.O.B:_____   Time:_____

Labor will last: ___Days ___Hours ___Mins

Guests

Name:_____

Parenting Advice

_____
_____
_____
_____

Wishes for Baby

_____
_____
_____
_____
_____

Resemblance

☐ Mostly Mom   ☐ Definitely Dad

I hope the baby gets Moms:_____

I hope the baby gets Dads:_____

Predictions

Eye Color: _____   Hair Color:_____

Length:_____   Weight:_____

D.O.B:_____   Time:_____

Labor will last: ___Days ___Hours ___Mins

Guests

Name:_____

Parenting Advice

_____

_____

_____

_____

_____

_____

Wishes for Baby

_____

_____

_____

_____

_____

Resemblance

☐ Mostly Mom   ☐ Definitely Dad

I hope the baby gets Moms:_____

I hope the baby gets Dads:_____

Predictions

Eye Color: _____   Hair Color:_____

Length:_____   Weight:_____

D.O.B:_____   Time:_____

Labor will last: ___Days ___Hours ___Mins

Guests

Name:_____

Parenting Advice

_____
_____
_____
_____
_____
_____

Wishes for Baby

_____
_____
_____
_____
_____

Resemblance

☐ Mostly Mom   ☐ Definitely Dad

I hope the baby gets Moms:_____

I hope the baby gets Dads:_____

Predictions

Eye Color: _____   Hair Color:_____

Length:_____   Weight:_____

D.O.B:_____   Time:_____

Labor will last: ___Days ___Hours ___Mins

Guests

Name:_____

Parenting Advice

_____
_____
_____
_____
_____
_____

Wishes for Baby

_____
_____
_____
_____
_____
_____

Resemblance

☐ Mostly Mom   ☐ Definitely Dad

I hope the baby gets Moms:_____

I hope the baby gets Dads:_____

Predictions

Eye Color: _____   Hair Color:_____

Length:_____   Weight:_____

D.O.B:_____   Time:_____

Labor will last: ___Days ___Hours ___Mins

Guests

Name:_____

Parenting Advice

Wishes for Baby

Resemblance

☐ Mostly Mom   ☐ Definitely Dad

I hope the baby gets Moms:_____

I hope the baby gets Dads:_____

Predictions

Eye Color: _____   Hair Color:_____

Length:_____   Weight:_____

D.O.B:_____   Time:_____

Labor will last: ___Days ___Hours ___Mins

Guests

Name:_____

Parenting Advice

_____
_____
_____
_____
_____
_____

Wishes for Baby

_____
_____
_____
_____

Resemblance

☐ Mostly Mom   ☐ Definitely Dad

I hope the baby gets Moms:_____

I hope the baby gets Dads:_____

Predictions

Eye Color: _____   Hair Color:_____

Length:_____   Weight:_____

D.O.B:_____   Time:_____

Labor will last: ___Days ___Hours ___Mins

Guests

Name:_____

Parenting Advice

Wishes for Baby

Resemblance

☐ Mostly Mom   ☐ Definitely Dad

I hope the baby gets Moms:_____

I hope the baby gets Dads:_____

Predictions

Eye Color: _____   Hair Color:_____

Length:_____   Weight:_____

D.O.B:_____   Time:_____

Labor will last: ___Days ___Hours ___Mins

Guests

Name:_____

Parenting Advice

_____
_____
_____
_____
_____
_____

Wishes for Baby

_____
_____
_____
_____
_____
_____

Resemblance

☐ Mostly Mom   ☐ Definitely Dad

I hope the baby gets Moms:_____

I hope the baby gets Dads:_____

Predictions

Eye Color: _____   Hair Color:_____

Length:_____   Weight:_____

D.O.B:_____   Time:_____

Labor will last: ___Days ___Hours ___Mins

Guests

Name:_____

Parenting Advice

_____
_____
_____
_____
_____
_____

Wishes for Baby

_____
_____
_____
_____
_____

Resemblance

☐ Mostly Mom   ☐ Definitely Dad

I hope the baby gets Moms:_____

I hope the baby gets Dads:_____

Predictions

Eye Color: _____   Hair Color:_____

Length:_____   Weight:_____

D.O.B:_____   Time:_____

Labor will last: ___Days ___Hours ___Mins

Guests

Name:_____

Parenting Advice

Wishes for Baby

Resemblance

☐ Mostly Mom   ☐ Definitely Dad

I hope the baby gets Moms:_____

I hope the baby gets Dads:_____

Predictions

Eye Color: _____   Hair Color:_____

Length:_____   Weight:_____

D.O.B:_____   Time:_____

Labor will last: ___Days ___Hours ___Mins

Guests

Name:_____

Parenting Advice

_____
_____
_____
_____
_____
_____

Wishes for Baby

_____
_____
_____
_____
_____

Resemblance

☐ Mostly Mom   ☐ Definitely Dad

I hope the baby gets Moms:_____

I hope the baby gets Dads:_____

Predictions

Eye Color: _____   Hair Color:_____

Length:_____   Weight:_____

D.O.B:_____   Time:_____

Labor will last: ___Days ___Hours ___Mins

Guests

Name:_____

Parenting Advice

_____
_____
_____
_____
_____
_____

Wishes for Baby

_____
_____
_____
_____
_____

Resemblance

☐ Mostly Mom   ☐ Definitely Dad

I hope the baby gets Moms:_____

I hope the baby gets Dads:_____

Predictions

Eye Color: _____   Hair Color:_____

Length:_____   Weight:_____

D.O.B:_____   Time:_____

Labor will last: ___Days ___Hours ___Mins

Guests

Name:_____

Parenting Advice

_____
_____
_____
_____
_____
_____

Wishes for Baby

_____
_____
_____
_____
_____

Resemblance

☐ Mostly Mom   ☐ Definitely Dad

I hope the baby gets Moms:_____

I hope the baby gets Dads:_____

Predictions

Eye Color: _____   Hair Color:_____

Length:_____   Weight:_____

D.O.B:_____   Time:_____

Labor will last: ___Days ___Hours ___Mins

Guests

Name:_____

Parenting Advice

_____
_____
_____
_____
_____
_____

Wishes for Baby

_____
_____
_____
_____
_____

Resemblance

☐ Mostly Mom   ☐ Definitely Dad

I hope the baby gets Moms:_____

I hope the baby gets Dads:_____

Predictions

Eye Color: _____   Hair Color:_____

Length:_____   Weight:_____

D.O.B:_____   Time:_____

Labor will last: ___Days ___Hours ___Mins

Guests

Name:_____

Parenting Advice

_____
_____
_____
_____
_____
_____

Wishes for Baby

_____
_____
_____
_____
_____

Resemblance

☐ Mostly Mom   ☐ Definitely Dad

I hope the baby gets Moms:_____

I hope the baby gets Dads:_____

Predictions

Eye Color: _____   Hair Color:_____

Length:_____   Weight:_____

D.O.B:_____   Time:_____

Labor will last: ___Days ___Hours ___Mins

Guests

Name:_____

Parenting Advice

_____
_____
_____
_____
_____
_____

Wishes for Baby

_____
_____
_____
_____
_____
_____

Resemblance

☐ Mostly Mom   ☐ Definitely Dad

I hope the baby gets Moms:_____

I hope the baby gets Dads:_____

Predictions

Eye Color: _____   Hair Color:_____

Length:_____   Weight:_____

D.O.B:_____   Time:_____

Labor will last: ___Days ___Hours ___Mins

Guests

Name:_____

Parenting Advice

Wishes for Baby

Resemblance

☐ Mostly Mom   ☐ Definitely Dad

I hope the baby gets Moms:_____

I hope the baby gets Dads:_____

Predictions

Eye Color: _____   Hair Color:_____

Length:_____   Weight:_____

D.O.B:_____   Time:_____

Labor will last: ___Days ___Hours ___Mins

Guests

Name:_____

Parenting Advice

_____
_____
_____
_____
_____
_____

Wishes for Baby

_____
_____
_____
_____
_____

Resemblance

☐ Mostly Mom   ☐ Definitely Dad

I hope the baby gets Moms:_____

I hope the baby gets Dads:_____

Predictions

Eye Color: _____   Hair Color:_____

Length:_____   Weight:_____

D.O.B:_____   Time:_____

Labor will last: ___Days ___Hours ___Mins

Guests

Name:_____

Parenting Advice

_____
_____
_____
_____
_____
_____

Wishes for Baby

_____
_____
_____
_____
_____

Resemblance

☐ Mostly Mom   ☐ Definitely Dad

I hope the baby gets Moms:_____

I hope the baby gets Dads:_____

Predictions

Eye Color: _____   Hair Color:_____

Length:_____   Weight:_____

D.O.B:_____   Time:_____

Labor will last: ___Days ___Hours ___Mins

Guests

Name:_____

Parenting Advice

_____
_____
_____
_____
_____
_____

Wishes for Baby

_____
_____
_____
_____
_____

Resemblance

☐ Mostly Mom　　　☐ Definitely Dad

I hope the baby gets Moms:_____

I hope the baby gets Dads:_____

Predictions

Eye Color: _____　　Hair Color:_____

Length:_____　　Weight:_____

D.O.B:_____　　Time:_____

Labor will last: ___Days ___Hours ___Mins

Guests

Name:_____

Parenting Advice

_____
_____
_____
_____
_____

Wishes for Baby

_____
_____
_____
_____
_____
_____

Resemblance

☐ Mostly Mom   ☐ Definitely Dad

I hope the baby gets Moms:_____

I hope the baby gets Dads:_____

Predictions

Eye Color: _____   Hair Color:_____

Length:_____   Weight:_____

D.O.B:_____   Time:_____

Labor will last: ___Days ___Hours ___Mins

Guests

Name:_____

Parenting Advice

_____
_____
_____
_____
_____
_____

Wishes for Baby

_____
_____
_____
_____
_____

Resemblance

☐ Mostly Mom   ☐ Definitely Dad

I hope the baby gets Moms:_____

I hope the baby gets Dads:_____

Predictions

Eye Color: _____   Hair Color:_____

Length:_____   Weight:_____

D.O.B:_____   Time:_____

Labor will last: ___Days ___Hours ___Mins

Guests

Name:_____

Parenting Advice

_____
_____
_____
_____
_____
_____

Wishes for Baby

_____
_____
_____
_____
_____

Resemblance

☐ Mostly Mom   ☐ Definitely Dad

I hope the baby gets Moms:_____

I hope the baby gets Dads:_____

Predictions

Eye Color: _____   Hair Color:_____

Length:_____   Weight:_____

D.O.B:_____   Time:_____

Labor will last: ___Days ___Hours ___Mins

Guests

Name:_____

Parenting Advice

_____
_____
_____
_____
_____

Wishes for Baby

_____
_____
_____
_____
_____

Resemblance

☐ Mostly Mom   ☐ Definitely Dad

I hope the baby gets Moms:_____

I hope the baby gets Dads:_____

Predictions

Eye Color: _____   Hair Color:_____

Length:_____   Weight:_____

D.O.B:_____   Time:_____

Labor will last: ___Days ___Hours ___Mins

Guests

Name:_____

Parenting Advice

_____
_____
_____
_____
_____

Wishes for Baby

_____
_____
_____
_____
_____

Resemblance

☐ Mostly Mom   ☐ Definitely Dad

I hope the baby gets Moms:_____

I hope the baby gets Dads:_____

Predictions

Eye Color: _____   Hair Color:_____

Length:_____   Weight:_____

D.O.B:_____   Time:_____

Labor will last: ___Days ___Hours ___Mins

Guests

Name:_____

Parenting Advice

Wishes for Baby

Resemblance

☐ Mostly Mom   ☐ Definitely Dad

I hope the baby gets Moms:_____

I hope the baby gets Dads:_____

Predictions

Eye Color: _____   Hair Color:_____

Length:_____   Weight:_____

D.O.B:_____   Time:_____

Labor will last: ___Days ___Hours ___Mins

Guests

Name:_____

Parenting Advice

_____
_____
_____
_____
_____
_____

Wishes for Baby

_____
_____
_____
_____
_____

Resemblance

☐ Mostly Mom   ☐ Definitely Dad

I hope the baby gets Moms:_____

I hope the baby gets Dads:_____

Predictions

Eye Color: _____   Hair Color:_____

Length:_____   Weight:_____

D.O.B:_____   Time:_____

Labor will last: ___Days ___Hours ___Mins

Guests

Name:_____

Parenting Advice

_____
_____
_____
_____
_____
_____

Wishes for Baby

_____
_____
_____
_____
_____
_____

Resemblance

☐ Mostly Mom   ☐ Definitely Dad

I hope the baby gets Moms:_____

I hope the baby gets Dads:_____

Predictions

Eye Color: _____   Hair Color:_____

Length:_____   Weight:_____

D.O.B:_____   Time:_____

Labor will last: ___Days ___Hours ___Mins

Guests

Name:_____

Parenting Advice

_____

_____

_____

_____

Wishes for Baby

_____

_____

_____

_____

_____

Resemblance

☐ Mostly Mom   ☐ Definitely Dad

I hope the baby gets Moms:_____

I hope the baby gets Dads:_____

Predictions

Eye Color: _____   Hair Color:_____

Length:_____   Weight:_____

D.O.B:_____   Time:_____

Labor will last: ___Days ___Hours ___Mins

Guests

Name:_____

Parenting Advice

Wishes for Baby

Resemblance

☐ Mostly Mom   ☐ Definitely Dad

I hope the baby gets Moms:_____

I hope the baby gets Dads:_____

Predictions

Eye Color: _____   Hair Color:_____

Length:_____   Weight:_____

D.O.B:_____   Time:_____

Labor will last: ___Days ___Hours ___Mins

Guests

Name:_____

Parenting Advice

_____
_____
_____
_____
_____
_____

Wishes for Baby

_____
_____
_____
_____
_____

Resemblance

☐ Mostly Mom   ☐ Definitely Dad

I hope the baby gets Moms:_____

I hope the baby gets Dads:_____

Predictions

Eye Color: _____   Hair Color:_____

Length:_____   Weight:_____

D.O.B:_____   Time:_____

Labor will last: ___Days ___Hours ___Mins

Guests

Name:_____

Parenting Advice

_____
_____
_____
_____
_____
_____

Wishes for Baby

_____
_____
_____
_____
_____
_____

Resemblance

☐ Mostly Mom   ☐ Definitely Dad

I hope the baby gets Moms:_____

I hope the baby gets Dads:_____

Predictions

Eye Color: _____   Hair Color:_____

Length:_____   Weight:_____

D.O.B:_____   Time:_____

Labor will last: ___Days ___Hours ___Mins

Gift log

Name: _____
Gift: _____
Thank You Sent: _____

Name: _____
Gift: _____
Thank You Sent: _____

Name: _____
Gift: _____
Thank You Sent: _____

Name: _____
Gift: _____
Thank You Sent: _____

Name: _____
Gift: _____
Thank You Sent: _____

Name: _____
Gift: _____
Thank You Sent: _____

Name: _____
Gift: _____
Thank You Sent: _____

Name: _____
Gift: _____
Thank You Sent: _____

Gift log

Name: _____
Gift: _____
Thank You Sent: _____

Name: _____
Gift: _____
Thank You Sent: _____

Name: _____
Gift: _____
Thank You Sent: _____

Name: _____
Gift: _____
Thank You Sent: _____

Name: _____
Gift: _____
Thank You Sent: _____

Name: _____
Gift: _____
Thank You Sent: _____

Name: _____
Gift: _____
Thank You Sent: _____

Name: _____
Gift: _____
Thank You Sent: _____

Gift log

Name: _____
Gift: _____
Thank You Sent: _____

Name: _____
Gift: _____
Thank You Sent: _____

Name: _____
Gift: _____
Thank You Sent: _____

Name: _____
Gift: _____
Thank You Sent: _____

Name: _____
Gift: _____
Thank You Sent: _____

Name: _____
Gift: _____
Thank You Sent: _____

Name: _____
Gift: _____
Thank You Sent: _____

Name: _____
Gift: _____
Thank You Sent: _____

Gift log

Name: _____
Gift: _____
Thank You Sent: _____

Name: _____
Gift: _____
Thank You Sent: _____

Name: _____
Gift: _____
Thank You Sent: _____

Name: _____
Gift: _____
Thank You Sent: _____

Name: _____
Gift: _____
Thank You Sent: _____

Name: _____
Gift: _____
Thank You Sent: _____

Name: _____
Gift: _____
Thank You Sent: _____

Name: _____
Gift: _____
Thank You Sent: _____

Gift Log

Name: _____
Gift: _____
Thank You Sent: _____

Name: _____
Gift: _____
Thank You Sent: _____

Name: _____
Gift: _____
Thank You Sent: _____

Name: _____
Gift: _____
Thank You Sent: _____

Name: _____
Gift: _____
Thank You Sent: _____

Name: _____
Gift: _____
Thank You Sent: _____

Name: _____
Gift: _____
Thank You Sent: _____

Name: _____
Gift: _____
Thank You Sent: _____

Gift log

Name: _____
Gift: _____
Thank You Sent: _____

Name: _____
Gift: _____
Thank You Sent: _____

Name: _____
Gift: _____
Thank You Sent: _____

Name: _____
Gift: _____
Thank You Sent: _____

Name: _____
Gift: _____
Thank You Sent: _____

Name: _____
Gift: _____
Thank You Sent: _____

Name: _____
Gift: _____
Thank You Sent: _____

Name: _____
Gift: _____
Thank You Sent: _____

Gift log

Name: _____
Gift: _____
Thank You Sent: _____

Name: _____
Gift: _____
Thank You Sent: _____

Name: _____
Gift: _____
Thank You Sent: _____

Name: _____
Gift: _____
Thank You Sent: _____

Name: _____
Gift: _____
Thank You Sent: _____

Name: _____
Gift: _____
Thank You Sent: _____

Name: _____
Gift: _____
Thank You Sent: _____

Name: _____
Gift: _____
Thank You Sent: _____

Gift log

Name: _____
Gift: _____
Thank You Sent: _____

Name: _____
Gift: _____
Thank You Sent: _____

Name: _____
Gift: _____
Thank You Sent: _____

Name: _____
Gift: _____
Thank You Sent: _____

Name: _____
Gift: _____
Thank You Sent: _____

Name: _____
Gift: _____
Thank You Sent: _____

Name: _____
Gift: _____
Thank You Sent: _____

Name: _____
Gift: _____
Thank You Sent: _____

Gift Log

Name: _____
Gift: _____
Thank You Sent: _____

Name: _____
Gift: _____
Thank You Sent: _____

Name: _____
Gift: _____
Thank You Sent: _____

Name: _____
Gift: _____
Thank You Sent: _____

Name: _____
Gift: _____
Thank You Sent: _____

Name: _____
Gift: _____
Thank You Sent: _____

Name: _____
Gift: _____
Thank You Sent: _____

Name: _____
Gift: _____
Thank You Sent: _____

Gift log

Name: _____
Gift: _____
Thank You Sent: _____

Name: _____
Gift: _____
Thank You Sent: _____

Name: _____
Gift: _____
Thank You Sent: _____

Name: _____
Gift: _____
Thank You Sent: _____

Name: _____
Gift: _____
Thank You Sent: _____

Name: _____
Gift: _____
Thank You Sent: _____

Name: _____
Gift: _____
Thank You Sent: _____

Name: _____
Gift: _____
Thank You Sent: _____

Gift log

Name: _____
Gift: _____
Thank You Sent: _____

Name: _____
Gift: _____
Thank You Sent: _____

Name: _____
Gift: _____
Thank You Sent: _____

Name: _____
Gift: _____
Thank You Sent: _____

Name: _____
Gift: _____
Thank You Sent: _____

Name: _____
Gift: _____
Thank You Sent: _____

Name: _____
Gift: _____
Thank You Sent: _____

Name: _____
Gift: _____
Thank You Sent: _____

Gift log

Name: _____
Gift: _____
Thank You Sent: _____

Name: _____
Gift: _____
Thank You Sent: _____

Name: _____
Gift: _____
Thank You Sent: _____

Name: _____
Gift: _____
Thank You Sent: _____

Name: _____
Gift: _____
Thank You Sent: _____

Name: _____
Gift: _____
Thank You Sent: _____

Name: _____
Gift: _____
Thank You Sent: _____

Name: _____
Gift: _____
Thank You Sent: _____

Made in United States
North Haven, CT
14 May 2022

19183702R00063